The Lure of Loch Lomond

A Journey Round the Islands and Environs

Ronald M.

Forth Naturalist and Historian

Published 1997 by the Forth Naturalist and Historian,
    University of Stirling
Honorary Editor/Secretary, L. Corbett

The Lure of Loch Lomond
ISBN 0 9514147 6 3

Cataloguing - in - publication data is available from the British Library

Cover - Paintings by E.W. Haslehust, 1922 - front, Ben Lomond from
    Luss, back - Luss Straights
Centre Photographs by K.J.H. Mackay

Camera readied (text 10pt. Palatino) by L. Corbett and
    Media Services, University of Stirling

Printed by Meigle Printers Ltd., Galashiels, on Crusader 100gms

CONTENTS

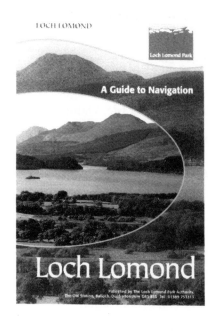

Ordnance Survey

Outdoor Leisure 39

Loch Lomond

Showing the West Highland Way
Ardlui to Milngavie

A leisure map of this popular area with tourist information

THE *Loch Lomond* ASSOCIATION
Code of Conduct

Enjoy Yourself and Go Safely

1:25 000 scale
4 cm to 1 km - 2½ in to 1 mile

The Loch Lomond Park Authority's *Guide to Navigation* and
Registration of Navigation Byelaws are from 1996 the official guides to and rules for the
behaviour of users of the waters for leisure and recreation. The *Code of Conduct* of the
Loch Lomond Association has been the general guide for many years. The *OS Outdoor
Leisure 39* is a very detailed large map scaled 2.5 to the mile.

FOREWORD

The contents of the following pages constitute a simple description of Loch Lomond and the islands, and endeavour to acquaint the visitor, casual or otherwise, on foot, awheel or on water, with her beauty, history, and legends, together with a few illustrative anecdotes. Regarded by many as Scotland's premier loch, it is the largest natural freshwater area in the British Isles, and at 630 feet the third deepest loch in Britain.

The construction of a control barrage on the River Leven in 1970 together with increasing rainfall levels, have resulted in a higher average depth than hitherto charted. A cold wet winter will cause a rise of several feet; consequently, a number of the smaller beaches and islets disappear at high water and many shoals and rocks lie just submerged. These fluctuating hazards are marked with an 'X' on the eight charts on pages 17 to 24. These charts are a helpful guide but weekend or touring sailors should get and use the Loch Lomond Park Authority's *Registration and Navigation Byelaws*, and *Guide to Navigation* for detailed instructions and information. The latter is a large (A2 folded) chart. Byelaws now in force are monitored by patrols and rangers. All boats must be registered, properly handled and speed controlled.

While sailing or exploring it should be borne in mind that not only is this Scotland's greatest freshwater loch, it is also a reservoir, and should be treated accordingly. Note also that the Islands are either privately owned or the property of the National Trust for Scotland, and Scottish Natural Heritage. The descriptions of the various localities are here kept brief but further study can be pursued in the publications listed in the bibliography, including those by enthusiasts such as Tom Weir and Jimmie MacGregor. Seekers of information on flora and fauna may refer to Glasgow University's *Natural History of Loch Lomond*, while visiting anglers should note that the Loch Lomond Angling Improvements Association holds all fishing rights to the Loch. There are Visitor/Information Centres at Balloch Old Station, Balloch Castle and at Luss village.

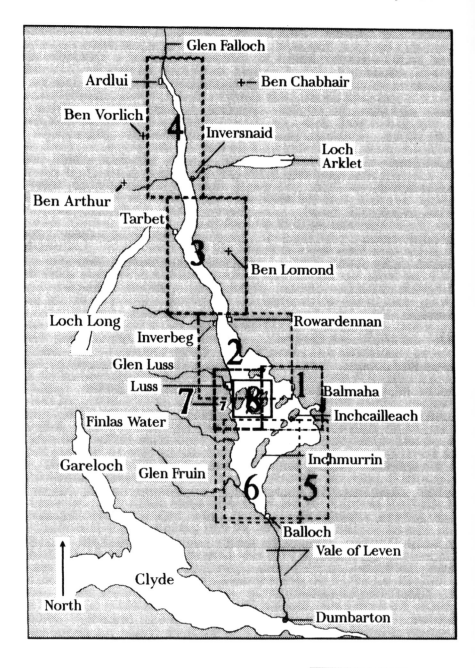

Charts 1-8 are on pages 17-24

Scale 5 miles = 8km

The First Marvel of Britain
Nennius (9th century)

When viewed from Ben Lomond, the emerald islands of the Loch lie strewn across her silver expanse like jewels in the crown of this queen of inland waters. The largest stretch of landlocked water in the country (being over 70 sq km/27 sq miles, 38 km/24 miles long and 8 km/c5 miles across at the widest point), she is undoubtedly one of nature's precious gifts. Her waters are dark and deep (190 m/600 feet/100 fathoms in places), and capable of raging like a furious sea when roused. Treat her with respect, and she will reward you with revelations of her beauty, mystery and wonders. Abuse her, or ignore her warning signals and she can become a dangerous enemy. Tranquil, she is enchanting, and, winter or summer, is a delight to all visitors. During the severe winter of 1895, when covered in thick ice, she allowed horse-drawn carts to carry goods to and from Balloch and Inchmurrin, and people were able to skate from Balloch to Luss.

The Loch was anciently known as 'Loch Levand' from the Vale and river of Leven, which is the only outlet from Balloch in the south to Dumbarton on the Clyde. Other sources claim that 'Lomond' derives from the dominating Ben Lomond akin to the other side of Scotland where Loch Leven is overlooked by the Lomond Hills. The Welsh historian Nennius (c800 AD), refers to the Loch as 'stagnum Lumonoy', and the river as 'Lemen' (Leven). 'Lluch Llemanawc' was an ancient British hero-god! and corruption of 'Lemanaux' links with the name of this whole area, the lands and Earldom of Lennox. Another source finds Lomond derived from 'Laoman' a hero of Celtic antiquity, and in his *Tours of 1760* Pennant refers to it as 'Lough Loughman'.

Most interesting of all, in his *The Marvels of Britain* Nennius calls the loch 'The first marvel of Britain'!

The East Bank from Balmaha to Glen Falloch

Balmaha to Strathcashell (Chart One - page 17)

A natural harbour on the east (Stirlingshire) shore of the loch, Balmaha is a delightful setting for the numerous pleasure craft moored here. The moored boats swing easily and securely, protected on the right by the high rock of Balmaha Pass (named from the 5th century St. Machar), and by the island of Inchcailleach a few hundred yards ahead at the entrance to the bay. Conic Hill rises 358m/1175feet behind, and with the south-western chain of islands, from Inchcailleach to Inchmurrin, forms part of the Highland Boundary Fault.

A rocky outcrop above the northern jetty known as Craigie Fourt may be the site of an iron-age fortification.

The shopping area and pub supply most requirements for visitors and boating enthusiasts, while small craft may be launched or hired at MacFarlane's Boatyard for a moderate fee, and many visitors and anglers make full use of this facility. MacFarlane's operate a Royal Mail service to the various inhabited islands, and a pleasure boat which plies regularly between Balmaha and Inchcailleach.

Inchcailleach

Having had the good fortune to explore each and every island and islet over many years we have come to know and love their individual charm. Every jewel has its own mystery and character, and a personal tale to tell, not least this 'Island of the cowled women' (a 1701 description names the island 'Ilan Carlah' or Carline, old Scots for the feminine of Carle - a man in his prime). It is reputed to be the burial place of St. Kentigerna (mother of St. Fillan), who died here in 733 AD. There are ruins of a 12th century religious building (probably built over the original 8th century edifice) and both ancient and comparatively recent burials in the old graveyard attest to continuity in its use. The Scottish droop-quilloned sword found sculpted on numerous West highland grave-slabs, along with much more ornamental and typically Celtic carving, may be seen here on the older tombstones. The sword-types date from the 14th/15th centuries. Tombstones bearing the names MacGregor and MacFarlane abound, including Rob Roy's ancestor Gregor MacGregor who was buried here in 1623. One headstone, dated 1783, bears the name Duncan MacFarlane, and is inscribed with the clan slogan 'Loch Sloy'.

Inchcailleach is undoubtedly the most beautiful, and certainly the most interesting of the nearby islands, almost a mile long and a half-mile wide. 'Tom na Nigheean' the 200 feet peak covered in pine-trees is the Gaelic for the 'Peak of the Women'. A restored eighteenth century corn-drying kiln is one of the many features on the Nature Trail. Good fishing is to be had all around, with salmon and sea-trout, while three and four foot pike have been caught. The best grounds for fly-fishing lie off the west banks. Nature Trail pamphlets containing a complete guide to the island are available at Balmaha and most information centres.

Portbawn and Torrinch

Perhaps the most delightful spot for the visitor to Inchcailleach is Portbawn, an enchanting little bay facing Torrinch (variously written 'Torremach' - 'Turrinig' - Towering Rock island), but a short distance south-west. Craggy Torrinch is covered in oaks, while the north-west grounds are replete with sea-trout and salmon. Off the west shore is a large rock known as 'The Stot'. Portbawn is a brilliant in the jewel of Inchcailleach, providing a pleasant little beach and greensward where the Nature Conservancy Wardens of the Loch have created an admirable picnic/camping ground, including seats and tables and an excellent barbecue fireplace, unfortunately, not always treated with the respect necessary to maintain its perpetuity. They are also responsible for the splendid two and a half miles of scenic Nature Trail, which is as pleasant as it is informative.

Old Pat was a regular camper at Portbawn, and every summer would arrive from some tenement close in Glasgow, hire a rowing boat from MacFarlane's (an outboard was too expensive), and row around to the lovely little bay. He pitched his small tent on the patch of greensward, and would remain here for the summer, rowing himself around the island each day; to return with his boat laden with driftwood and fallen timber for the campfire. He made all visitors welcome and was always good for a cup of tea and a chat.

I don't know if he communed with the white hind which frequents this island; she usually appeared as a ghostly figure between the trees, just outside the peripheral glow of the flickering campfire. But the squirrels loved him. He called them 'pestiferous beasties' yet he would leave a little gap in a corner of his tent before rowing off on his foraging.

He also deliberately left a previously opened packet of biscuits or nuts there. His tent is no longer seen in Portbawn, and the squirrels are not quite so tuned in to humans as they were when Pat from Glasgow spent his summers there. It was said that he'd been mugged on the streets of his city, beaten up for the sake of the few pence he had on him. I don't know if he had anyone to care for him. The squirrels missed him and, perhaps, still do.

Clairinch and the Kitchen

Called 'Flat Island' this lies just south-east off Inchcailleach and is a quarter mile long and heavily wooded. The unexcavated ruins of a number of very ancient buildings are completely overgrown, and it is interesting to find that one early name for this island was 'Illan nam Claoimha' or Isle of Sword(s)', which Clairinch may be a corruption of - 'Claimh Ins', for 'Clairinch' is the ancient slogan of the Buchanans, whose territory is all around. The ruins of a large oblong building and paved hut-circles stand at the north-eastern point. Archaeological finds indicate that this is the site of an iron-age settlement. Also intriguing is the tiny crannog off the north-eastern tip known as the Kitchen or 'Ceap na hinseig', literally 'Knob of the islet', where Roman pottery was discovered in recent years. Early registers name this tiny islet 'Kepnichek' or 'Knap Mhichag', examples of the frequent mistakes which occur when the Gaelic is set down phonetically.

The Regional boundary of Central (Stirlingshire), and Strathclyde (Glasgow), runs midway between the narrow passage separating Inchcailleach and Torrinch. Both line up with Creinch and Inchmurrin in a south-west line which marks the Highland Boundary Fault, a dislocation of the earth's crust which threw up this line of rocks millions of years ago. The line runs from Stonehaven in the north-east to Kintyre in the south-west.

Arrochymore

Once over the Pass of Balmaha, steep and narrow, the road to Rowardennan winds down to a pleasant little beach just before Arrochymore Point, where cars may be parked on the smooth grassy field for the day (at a small charge) and small dinghies or canoes are easily launched. Ideal for a picnic.

Inchfad

'Innis fhada' - Long Island - the third of the islands within the shire Stirling boundary, lies just off Arrochymore Point. Low-lying and grassy, fringed with alders and hazels, it is also one of the sunniest. There is a small farm-house with rolling pastureland covering the eastern three-quarters. Inchfad is over a mile long, a quarter mile wide, a mile from Balmaha pier, half a mile round from Arrochymore Point. There is excellent fishing water all round. Record size fly-caught salmon have been landed off the western tip. The average depth between here and Inchcruin is 18ft/5.5m. A buoy marks a large clump of occasionally visible rock called 'Little Ireland'. Between this and Inchcruin the depth averages 12ft/3.6m. Off the south-west tip lies Ellenderroch - Oak Island - from the large oak trees on this crescent-shaped islet which is much favoured by the angling fraternity.

Milarrochy Bay

A half-mile further and the road runs alongside Milarrochy Bay, a lovely wooded area where a flat shingle beach is the scene of much summer activity, and where power-boats and other small craft may be launched from the trailer. Unfortunately this ideal spot is not always treated with the respect it deserves. From here a road follows the shore-line to the so-called Canoe Club (actually a prestigious sailing club), where a variety of fast sail-boats frequently compete in well-organised races. Boaters are warned that the sail-boats have right of way, and should be kept well clear of when a race is in progress.

Next on the B837 is the Caravan Club site and moorings and, in another mile or so, the very popular, well-kept Forestry commission camp site which covers most of the Point of Strathcashell.

Strathcashell to Rowardennan (Chart Two - page 18)

Strathcashell

Here, at the Forestry Commission's excellent site in Queen Elizabeth Forest Park, small-craft may be launched from the beach. There is also a small jetty. Cashell is a corruption of the Latin 'Castellum' which indicates that the tumbled stones on the point are the remains of an early fortified structure with, perhaps, some connections with St. Kessog. Not far away in Callander a mound covering the remains of his church is known as 'Tom na Kessaig', and his feast is still celebrated as 'Feill na Chessaig' on 10th March.

The area covered by the ruins at Strathcashell is c 700m^2, and includes single identifiable building (Glasgow University, p85). It was once known as the 'Giants Castle' (a mistaken translation of an old name 'Rownafean' or Point of the Fiann/Men).

Just off the point are the once well-preserved and substantial oak foundations of a crannog, a man-made lake-dwelling, a number of which are scattered around the loch. Now overgrown, this was listed as Ilan a Cashil in 1701.

Inchlonaig

'Inchlonachie' - Island of marshes - also known as 'The Yew-Tree Island' lies half mile west from Strathcashell, three quarters from Luss, and is almost a mile long, a half-mile wide and 200 feet/62m high. The dark forest of ancient Yew Trees was (according to tradition) re-planted by Bruce after using it to supply bow-wood for his army. A 1506 Chartulary mentions a payment to a 'Clarscha' (Harper) on the island, but for what purpose remains unknown, presumably during some celebratory event. It was converted to a Deer Park of the Colquhoun Lairds of Luss in 1630, and supported a herd of 150 deer. The family inhabiting the farmhouse and working the lands during the 18th century are reputed to have taken in as boarders - 'persons much given to intoxication', presumably to dry them out and persuade them from their evil ways. The 'seven public-houses' of Luss Parish quoted in 1796 (see section covering Luss) were no doubt partially responsible! High and rocky, the east shore provides a magnificent variety of contours and foliage. Ruins of ancient lime-kilns are situated on the small promontory in the southern bay facing Inchconnachan, with a house situated nearby. Sir James Colquhoun and his shooting party were drowned while returning to Luss from a deer hunt on Inchlonaig on 18th December 1873. Their memorial stands in the old churchyard at Luss.

Remains belonging to the mesolithic (Middle Stone-Age), period have been found on the eastern shores, and some of the best fishing grounds on the loch off the north shore. South and midway between the island and Inchconnachan lies Sharbau Bank, shoals indicated by a marker-buoy.

Isles of the Ross

Continuing up the east shore we have a mile and a half of sweeping bay of Rowardennan Forest (the western part of the great 'Queen Elizabeth Forest Park of the Lomond/Trossachs area. The sailor may now coast northward towards the great promontory of Ross Point and Ross Wood, wherein lies 'Lochain Dubh' - the 'black pool' - adjacent to the Research Station of the Universities of Glasgow and Stirling. 'Losgainn Bay' lies below, before the loch narrows to less than a mile from Ross Point to Culag on the west bank.

Now we have the chain of 'Isles of the Ross' extending from Ross point. A number of pleasant little bays and beaches lie behind these rocky islets and around the point. The small wooded islet almost in mid-channel is 'Durrinch' which is sheer rock, and best avoided. It is described on the old charts as a 'Pilot Rock' for larger vessels. The larger 'Iland Dearg' (Red Island), is a beautiful little spot full of character, with excellent fishing (sea-trout and salmon) all around, but these Ross Isles should be kept clear of in contrary winds.

Montrose Bank

Beyond Ross Point the banks steepen as the loch narrows, and the water deepens accordingly. Situated between the Point and Rowardennan the frequently submerged peak of 'Montrose Bank' should be looked out for off the 'Mill of Ross', and the 'Mill Cairn'. Midway between the Point of Rowardennan and Inverbeg, the shoals of 'Inverbeg Bank' are marked by a beacon, and due east, opposite, is the private bay and beach of 'Port na Croibhe'. Access to Rowardennan Hotel is best from the main beach, or the car park. From the pier the ferry plies to Inverbeg three quarters of a mile away on the west bank. 'Ilan Rowardennan' lies ahead.

Rowardennan to Inversnaid (Charts Two and Three)

About half a mile beyond the ferry and pier the east shore B837 road ends at Ardess and the popular Youth Hostel. The walker may take the four mile well-marked path up to the 3,194ft (974m) summit of Ben Lomond where, weather permitting, the view is spectacular, even to include the coast of Ireland on a very clear day!

But do not try to emulate the minister of Aberfoyle who in July/August 1906 noted that it was possible to sit on top of Ben Lomond "in a serene atmosphere" and "observe a thunder cloud roll below, while lightning flashed between it and the lake beneath". The stout-hearted may also take the loch-side track (part of the West Highland Way) to Ptarmigan Lodge and Inversnaid.

Ilan Rou Ardennan (E. Deargannan)

Said to be named from a 'red dye' or the 'char' (a reddish trout), this small fir-covered island in this lovely bay provides shelter for the pier. Although currently named Deargannan (as Admiralty chart 1861), in 1701 it was I think listed more suitably as Ilan Rou Ardennan.

Hunter Bank, Stanley Rocks

North of Eilean Deargannan lies Hunter Bank - the 'Creaga Coorach' - submerged rocks lying off the pier, and west and slightly north are the Stanley Rocks lying mid-channel between the Youth Hostel, and Inverbeg Point on the west bank. Another mile north brings Ptarmigan Lodge, from where the ascent is the steepest to Ben Lomond towering above. The West Highland Way continues 5 miles from here to Inversnaid then on to Inverarnan another 6 miles . This east bank area, opposite Tarbet on the west bank is Craig Rostan, Rob Roy's territory, and just before the headland of Rowchoish, Rob Roy's 'Prison', a rock cell overhanging the loch, is seen on the right (by the sailor), or by a climb down by the walker. Several crannogs are believed to lie semi-submerged along the shores below Rowchoish, where a pleasant beach affords a landing, though submerged rocks and shoals should be carefully looked out for. Round the Point, the next beaching point is Cailness, between Craig Buchan and Cruachan, with Cruinn à Bheinn looming above. The loch depth plummets here to 105 fathoms (630ft/192m). Another mile and a half brings Inversnaid.

Inversnaid to Glen Falloch (Chart Four - page 20)

Inversnaid, Falls and the Garrison

The harbour and steamer pier (a ferry plies between here and Inveruglas on the west bank), and the bay north provide a reasonably sheltered anchorage here. The Inversnaid Hotel serves up excellent fare, and fuel and stores may be had. Coaches ply regularly between here and

Loch Katrine, Aberfoyle and Stirling. The Falls of Inversnaid just before the harbour provide a splendid and pleasurable walk/climb. We have often seen otters sporting here around the falls. Less than a mile uphill is 'The Garrison', the military barracks built in 1718-19 to hold two companies of red-coats, urged by Montrose to police the MacGregor country and capture Rob Roy.

Although well known, and detailed studies are available elsewhere, the story of the 1715 'Expedition' is worth recounting. In September 1715, the MacGregors plundered lands and shores for supplies obeying Lord Mar's appeal at the outbreak of the Jacobite Rising. In reprisal, 100 sailors from Naval vessels in the Clyde, together with volunteers from nearby towns, were shipped in the 'Men o' War' boats and towed by horses up the Leven. Joined at Luss by Sir Humphrey Colquhoun and James Grant (his son-in-law) with 50 "stately fellows in short hose and belted plaids, with guns, spiked targets, sturdy claymores; each with a pistol or two, and a knife and a durk in his belt", all went on to meet overland parties at Rowardennan, where, after firing a ball into a hut, they found only a few 'old wives'. They then "beat their drums for an hour", but no enemy appeared. "They chanced on the boats hidden by the MacGregors, took some, sank the rest, and returned home in triumph." There ended the 'Expedition'.

The Garrison, subsequently rebuilt, is now part of Inversnaid farm, and the graveyard contains tombstones to the men and women of various regiments who died while stationed here, 1721/1796.

Rob Roy's Cave

A mile beyond Inversnaid, Rob Roy's Cave (also known as Bruce's Cave) may be seen high on the hill on the right and on top of the rock immediately above is Sgiath an Righ - 'Shield of the King' (The Bruce), the rocks where the hero took shelter during the retreat after the battles of Methven, and Dalrigh in 1306. The whole area contains the ruins of many MacGregor homesteads, and a number of the primitive iron-smelting sites known as 'Bloomeries'. Almost two miles north lies Isle I Vow.

The steep and rocky banks below Beinn a' Choin are both awesome and magnificent, and there is little opportunity for anchorage or beaching on the east bank, until Ardliesh and Ardlui at the head of the loch.

Isle I Vow

Lying between Ben Vorlich to the west and the looming east bank below Beinn a' Choin to the east, the single acre-sized I Vow is some two miles from the mouth of the river Falloch at the head of the loch. It has received a variety of names - 'Ilan na Bochd' (Island of the Cell?) in 1701, the Wordsworths possibly refer to this in describing The Brownie's Cell (see Appendix One); 'Eilean a'Bogha' ('Island of the Bow') thus recognisable in view of the defensive nature of the castle; 'Elanvow' in 1364, the contracted colloquial Gaelic, 'I' pronounced 'Eehi'; a Gaelic poem of 1507, set down phonetically, quotes "Cha nee lesh a hideyn ny lesh e Vhow" - neither with his arrows or his bow, and might seem to settle the question in favour of Isle of the Bow. However when called 'Isle of Voles', this describes one of its most unusual aspects.

The island does seem to be filled with tiny black furry creatures scurrying about on their business. Vegetarians, these bewitching and bewhiskered little animals have black-button eyes and nose, and must not be confused with the rat family. It could be that the island should be named Elan na Vole. The voles are clannish by nature and communities of fifty or so appear to be usual. A 9th century poem from the Lismore Collection mentions dark-blue

mice (voles?) from Luimneach' (Lomond/Lumonoy/ Leamhnacht or Lennox) and I Vow springs to mind.

The Chief of Clann na' Vole is a bold inquisitive little fellow with whiskers. He and all his followers wore soft black velvet coats, and were round and plump, apparently very well fed. Their lack of fear of humans was most rewarding and satisfying.

A very small rock-cut jetty lies on the island's south-side, a large oblong rock providing access from a beached dinghy. On this southern end, the ruins of the ancient stronghold of the MacFarlanes may still be seen. Now covered in trees, the castle was in very good order when Eilean Vow was described by Buchanan of Auchmar c1710 as "a pretty good house with gardens".

Moving on northwards, the surrounding hills steepen sharply, especially as they narrow to their closest point just beyond I Vow, where we have in half a mile on the west bank the promentary Rubha Ban. On course to Ardlui and a little offshore lies a shoal which should be avoided by deep-draught vessels when the water level is low.

Glen Falloch

Some two miles on is the head of the loch, and beautiful bay at the mouth of the river Falloch. The Geal Loch (Clear/Bright Water) is formed by the silting from the River Falloch, and the channel and flatlands may be explored by small craft. Roughly one mile north, in Glen Falloch, is Inverarnan with its Hotel and long history of cattle droves and drovers, prehistoric carved stones, and stone circles. To see the ancient boundary-stone known as 'Clach nam Breatann' (Stone of the Britons), you must hike three quarters of a mile up the glen to beyond the Falls, where this marker-stone stands on a hillside at the eastern point of Dalriadan territory, and the southern terminus of the Grampians.

Under a more recent name - the 'Mortar Stone', it marks the reputed site where King Robert the Bruce regathered his strength after the engagement with the Lord of Lorn in 1306 at Dalrigh (Vale of the King) in Strathfillan, during which he lost the fabulous 'Brooch of Lorn'.

The stone commemorates a defeat of the Britons of Strathclyde (whose north-west border included all of the Lennox and Dunbartonshire in the 8th century), and the Scots of Dalriada (Argyll), whose eastermost point reached the Falloch. The site was also the south-western border of Pictland, where the *Annals* (Chambers 1874) list many battles. The defeat occurred in 717 AD shortly after the Pictish King Nechtan had "expelled the community of Iona across Drumalbain" (the southern reach of the Grampians). The laconic entry in the *Annals* reads: "717 AD: Conflict between the Dalriati and Britonum, at the stone called Minvircc, and the Britons were defeated." The Britons were possibly a coalition with the Picts, for the Christian community was back on Iona by 718 AD! Minvircc appears to be hybrid Pictish or Cymric, indicating Rim of Flatland - 'Limit of Habitat' or 'Mountain Edge', all suitably descriptive for this convergence of mountains.

Now damaged, the stone (a type called 'Clach an Brath' = Stone of Judgement/Destiny), points to the historical significance of the Loch, for it was a marker before the battle took place in 717 AD.   An ancient overland trail from Glen Fyne , the Larig Arnan, leads directly to this spot, and another now a well used section of the West Highland Way, leads on by the Falloch to Crianlarich.   The so-called 'Stepping-stones' over the River Falloch, are the remains of a medieval 'clapper-bridge'. They are now several feet under, and attest to the rise in the water-level. Fishing around the head of the Loch is mostly for the predatory pike.

The East Bank Southwards: Balmaha to Balloch

Balmaha to Balloch (Chart Five)

By the A837 eash shore road it is 3 miles to the A811 through Drymen to Balloch at the south end of Loch Lomond. We take the Loch route.

Loch Lomond Nature Reserve

From Balmaha, leaving Inchcailleach on our right, the lower flood plain of the River Endrick provides acres of grassland, shallow water and marshland, forming part of the Loch Lomond Nature Reserve. Terns, gulls, waders, herons, ducks and many other birds (ospreys have been sighted), gather to feed in the marshy vegetation, while flora and fauna are a treasurehouse to the naturalist. Here the Salmon run upstream for some twenty miles, with excellent spawning grounds, and the 'Leap' at the Pot of Gartness, is duly famous. Near Muirpark, Milton of Buchanan, is St. Machar's Well, well of the saint of Balmaha.

Torrinch

Lying just off Inchcailleach south-west of Portbawn, this precipitous rocky island rises sheer to 100 feet. A half mile long, and some 200 yards in width, it was once heavily wooded with Scots Firs until these were destroyed by fire. Oaks now grow in their place. A small area of gravel beach faces Portbawn, while just offshore to the west stands a small and bare rock named The Stot.

Aber Isle

Inshore from Torrinch, this 'Isle of the River-mouth' lies half a mile to the south of the River Endrick estuary, and slightly more north of Ross Priory. Once described as "a beautiful speck on the water" it is merely the tip of a much larger island, now mostly washed away. It has good fishing all round. It is part of the Lomond Nature Reserve as is Creinch one and a half miles to the west.

Ross Priory

Inland from the Pumping Station and once a seat of the Buchanans, Ross Priory was originally a monastery. It is now owned and used for social functions by Strathclyde University. Sir Walter Scott was a frequent visitor, and there, inspired by the scenery and folklore wrote parts of *Lady of the Lake* and *Rob Roy*. The Gardens are open on one day in May every year.

Port of Aber

Just to the east of Ross Priory, a few cultivated roses and a stone-paved road are almost all that remains of this deserted village. Fine red sandstone was quarried and ferried to Balloch on its way to Glasgow until both trade and village died during the late eighteenth century.

The inshore water between here and Balmaha is extremely shallow, and subject to sudden shoaling. Great care should be taken by vessels with all but shallow draught.

Gartocharn

Inland, on the A811, and beside the prominent Tom Weir famed, cone of basalt rock known as Duncryne which rises 142m/465 feet behind, this is a lovely village. Names here are a splendid mix of Cymric, Gaelic, Scandinavian, and Anglo-Saxon. Gartocharn means house and lands (garth) of 'Place of the Carn/Cairn'. Duncryne is nicknamed 'The Dumpling', a name that does little justice to this haunt of the so-called 'Colquhoun Fairies' - the 'sidhe' (pronounced shee), who were reputed to be the original occupants. The hill, however, is undoubtedly named from the 'Cruithne', frequently equated with the Picts, and/or the 'fairy shean'.

Creinch

'Tree Island' or Pict's Island, this heavily wooded island one and a half miles north-west of Ross Priory is roughly a quarter mile square, lying between the northern tip of Inchmurrin and Torrinch to the north-east. A large rock known as Prince of Wales Rock lies submerged just off the southern tip. Off-shore, to the east of the northern tip, stands a bare rock, similarly known like that off Torrinch, as The Stot. Sea-trout are commonly fished here.

Shore and Woods - Loch Lomond Nature Reserve

Northwards from Gartocharn and the A811 road, this area is a magnificent setting for naturalists but the casual visitor is advised to obtain permission first.

Port na Ellen Islets

Now mostly reefs and boulders overgrown with shrub, but once a busy spot, these lie offshore from East Portnellen Farm, opposite Inchmurrin. The southern-most islet is Yl Vealich Balloch (Isle of the Village on the Loch). The area is surrounded by shallows, and it is possible that this too was a port where the red sandstone was actually loaded for transport by barge to Balloch.

Inchmurrin

This one and half miles long island is well wooded and provides excellent pastureland, while supporting many deer. Barbed and stemmed flint arrowheads have been found here. Ancient monastic ruins lie below the northern 89m high Tom Buy (Yellow Peak) at the north-eastern end and are known as the 'Chappell of St. Mirren'. At the south-western tip are the ruins of Lennox Castle, a stronghold of the Earls of Lennox, near which stood a large deer-hunting lodge below Black Hill, built by the Montrose family in 1793. Isabella, Countess of Lennox, retired here in 1425 after her father, husband and two sons, lost their heads to the executioner. The isle was renowned for its whisky which found a ready market in Glasgow until the authorities launched an excise cutter. No doubt there were skirmishes, for the cutter was armed. Early in the 1715 Rising, it was sacked by the MacGregors and everything carried off to Inversnaid (see p9 the 'Expedition'). This island, in common with several others was known as a refuge for those with troubled minds, and in particular for "those of the fair sex who were unfortunate enough to give pregnant proof of their frailty"!

The Inchmurrin Boatel is a resort for anglers and boaters, while north and south are excellent sea-trout waters, and favourable for the salmon. A large jetty provides comfortable access unless overcrowded.

Boturich Castle

Another seat of the Buchanans, the present castle was built in 1834 on the site of Old Boturich Castle immortalised as a seat of the Lady Gleneagles by Sir David Lindsay in verse around 1550 entitled 'The Squyer o' Meldrum'. The Lady of Gleneagles is romantically engaged with the Squyer at her usual residence in Strathearn, where news arrives that the MacFarlanes have seized Boturich and are raiding the district. Meldrum immediately dons his armour, and with his men rides to expel them. After a bitter siege and struggle, he finally succeeds. Two lines in this rather long poem appear to say it all:

"And sae this Squyer Amorous; Seigit and wan the Ladies Hous;" It seems needless to say that he had previously won her heart, and that this gallant action brought him even closer ties!

On the shoreline before Balloch Castle, is a fisherman's 'marker', a glacial erratic (stone) variously called Patties, Patey,Pettie; a boundary-stone, terminal limit of Paternus a 5th century king of the southern Picts.

Balloch

Balloch Castle built by Buchanan of Ardoch in 1808 is now a Country Park, visitor centre, the Countryside Rangers Service, and 200 acres of parkland. A 'tulip-tree' grows among the copper-beeches.

Between the Balloch park and Cameron/Drumkinnon Bay to the west the loch water now funnels rapidly towards the River Leven, the loch's only outlet, passing through Balloch Marina towards Dumbarton and the Clyde. Balloch village is the centre for cruise boats, railway, visitor's information, hotels.

Further south in Vale of Leven lie several neolithic, bronze-age, and iron-age sites, no doubt the scene of many battles between the Picts, the Scots of Dalriada, and the Strathclyde Britons. The *Annals* record - "AD 704: the slaughter of the Dalriads in the vale of Lemna (Leven)".

Dunbarton - Fortress of the Britons

The *Annals* inform us this ancient 'Alclyde' was destroyed in AD780: "The burning of Alclutha on the Kalends of January." This destruction was possibly carried out by the Picts, for Scotland north of the Forth and Clyde, including Dunadd, the capital of the Dalriadan Scots, appears to have fallen into Pictish hands at this time. Castle and town are now spelled with 'm' but the shire with 'n'.

Dunbarton was repeatedly assailed during the evolutionary years of the Scottish state (the seventh to the ninth centuries). Kenneth MacAlpine became ruler of a united kingdom between the Picts and Scots from the Mearns to the Clyde in 843, 27 years later the Rock finally fell to the Northern 'Gentiles' (Danes) from occupied Dublin.

In AD870, Dunbarton was besieged by two 'Northmen Kings', Olaf and Ivor. After a long and bloody siege, the Northmen "destroyed the citadel, and plundered". This was undoubtedly a great disaster, for in 871, they returned to Dublin "with 200 ships and a great booty of men, Angles, Britons and Picts ... into captivity."

This last mention is interesting as one of the earliest notices concerning a possible amalgamation or coalition of Britons, Scots and Picts. The term 'Scots' is noticeably absent, the Dalriadans retaining their title for some years, before becoming 'Albanich'. It is not until the tenth century that the Picts and Dalriadans merged under this collective as inhabitants of Alban = Scotland, the kingdom even then only covering the Clyde, Argyll, West Stirlingshire, Perthshire and Angus. Most of north Alban was still held by a few rulers of individual kingdoms, while the greater part of what is now southern Scotland was held by Northumbrian Kings.

Lying at the very heart of this great new nation was Loch Lomond!

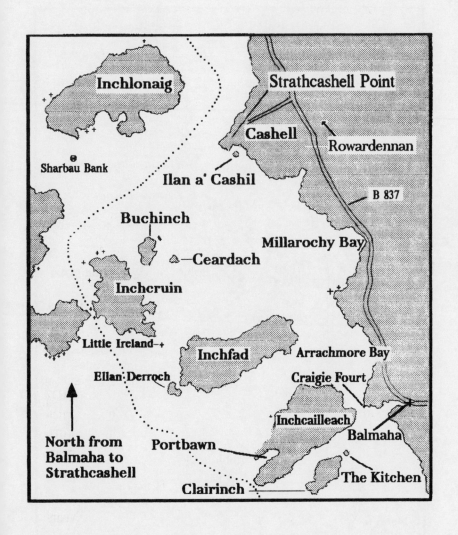

Scale: 1 mile = 1.6km

Chart One - Northwards: Balmaha to Strathcashell

+ = shoals or submerged rocks   Dotted line = Central Region/Dumbarton Boundary

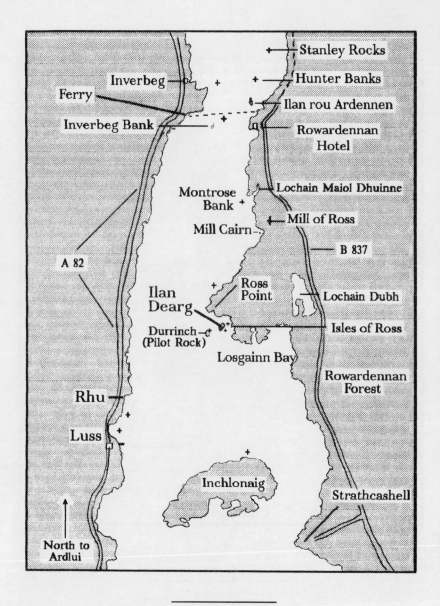

Stanley Rocks

Hunter Banks

Inverbeg

Ferry

Ilan rou Ardennen

Inverbeg Bank

Rowardennan
Hotel

Lochain Maiol Dhuinne

Montrose
Bank

Mill of Ross

Mill Cairn

B 837

A 82

Ross
Point

Ilan
Dearg

Lochain Dubh

Durrinch
(Pilot Rock)

Isles of Ross

Losgainn Bay

Rowardennan
Forest

Rhu

Luss

Inchlonaig

Strathcashell

North to
Ardlui

Scale: 1 mile = 1.6km

Chart Two - Northwards: Strathcashell to Rowardennan (East Bank)
Luss to Inverbeg (West Bank)

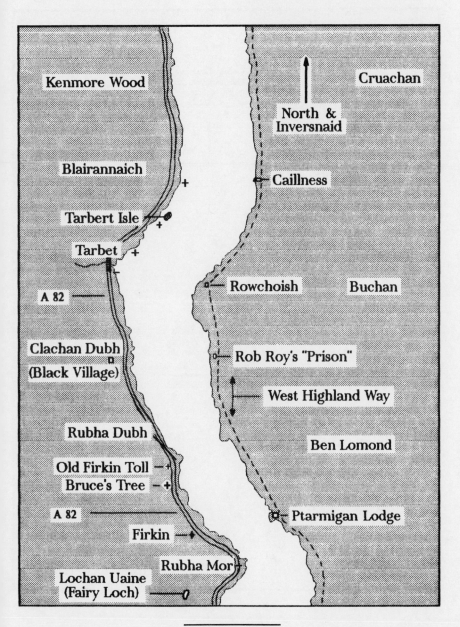

Kenmore Wood

Cruachan

North &
Inversnaid

Blairannaich

Caillness

Tarbert Isle

Tarbet

A 82

Rowchoish

Buchan

Clachan Dubh
(Black Village)

Rob Roy's "Prison"

West Highland Way

Rubha Dubh

Ben Lomond

Old Firkin Toll
Bruce's Tree

A 82

Ptarmigan Lodge

Firkin

Rubha Mor

Lochan Uaine
(Fairy Loch)

Scale: 1 mile = 1.6km

Chart Three - Northwards: Rowardennan to Inversnaid (East Bank)

Inverbeg to Tarbet (West Bank)

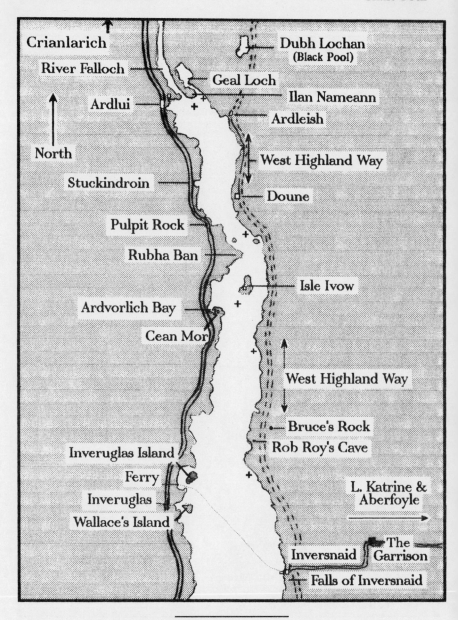

Crianlarich

River Falloch

Ardlui

North

Stuckindroin

Pulpit Rock

Rubha Ban

Ardvorlich Bay

Cean Mor

Inveruglas Island

Ferry

Inveruglas

Wallace's Island

Dubh Lochan
(Black Pool)

Geal Loch

Ilan Nameann

Ardleish

West Highland Way

Doune

Isle Ivow

West Highland Way

Bruce's Rock

Rob Roy's Cave

L. Katrine &
Aberfoyle

The
Garrison

Inversnaid

Falls of Inversnaid

Scale: 1 mile = 1.6km

Chart Four - Northwards: Inversnaid to Glen Falloch (East Bank)

Tarbet to Inveruglas and Ardlui (West Bank)

Sunset at Balmaha

Inchcailleach from
Craigie Fort, Balmaha

Inchcailleach summit:
Geggle of isles: distant
Luss hills

These photographs relate to p2 of the text.

(a)

Inchfad from
Millarrochy Bay

Dinghy sails in sunset

Loch Lomond from
Duncryne

The first two photographs relate to p5, the third to pp 12/13 of text.

(b)

Inchmurrin and site of
Castle of Lennox

Yew tree and south
coast of Inchloanaig

Shore of Inchmoan:
Narrows -
Inchtavannach
(l)/Inchconnachan (r)
narrows

These photographs relate to pp 14, 26 and 31 respectively in the text.

Activity on the west
beach, Inchmoan

Narrows-
Inchtavannach/Inchcon
nachan looking
towards the Ben

Ben Vane Inveruglus
Glen, Loch Sloy
power station (r),
taken from the
Inversnaid ferry

These photographs relate to pp 31, 34 and 38 respectively in the text.

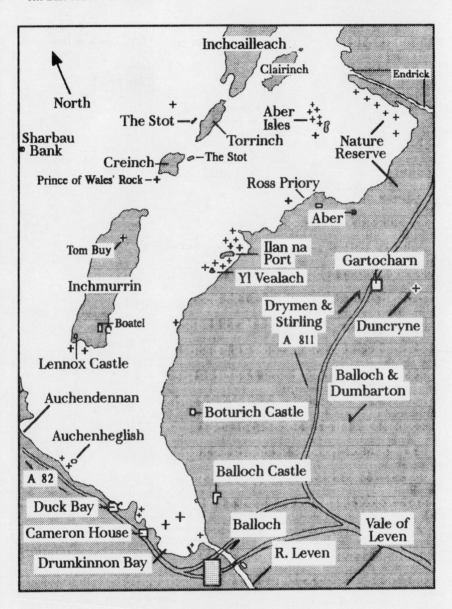

North

Inchcailleach

Clairinch

Endrick

The Stot

Aber Isles

Nature Reserve

Sharbau Bank

Torrinch

Creinch — The Stot

Prince of Wales' Rock

Ross Priory

Aber

Tom Buy

Ilan na Port

Gartocharn

Inchmurrin

Yl Vealach

Drymen & Stirling

A 811

Duncryne

Boatel

Balloch & Dumbarton

Lennox Castle

Auchendennan

Boturich Castle

Auchenheglish

Balloch Castle

A 82

Duck Bay

Balloch

Vale of Leven

Cameron House

R. Leven

Drumkinnon Bay

Scale: 1 mile = 1.6km

Chart Five - Southwards: Balmaha to Balloch (East Bank)

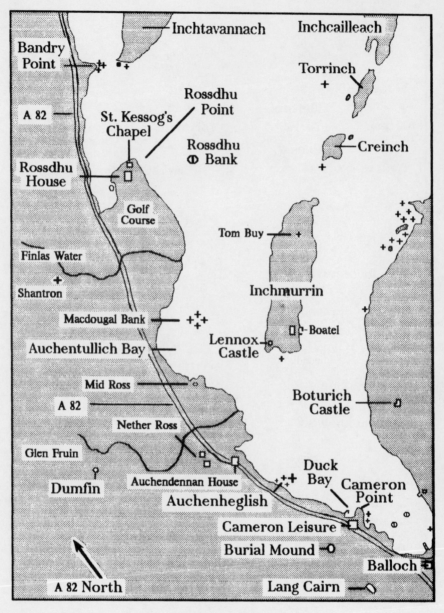

Scale: 1 mile = 1.6km

Chart Six - Northwards: Balloch to Bandry Point (West Bank)

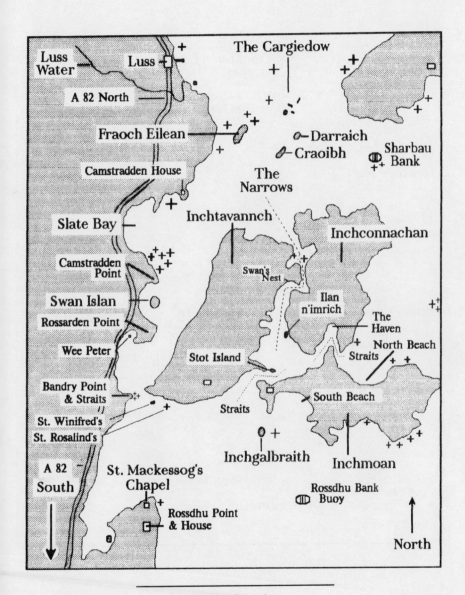

Scale: 1mile = 1.6km

Chart Seven - Northwards: Bandry Point via Camstradden Sound to Luss

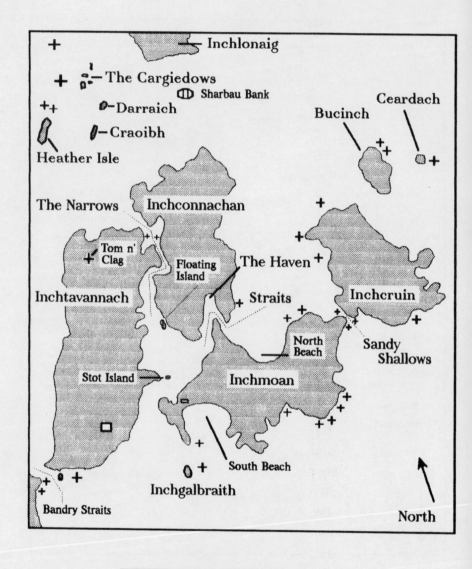

Inchlonaig

The Cargiedows

Sharbau Bank

Darraich

Ceardach

Bucinch

Craoibh

Heather Isle

The Narrows   Inchconnachan

Tom n' Clag

Floating Island   The Haven

Inchcruin

Inchtavannach   Straits

North Beach   Sandy Shallows

Stot Island   Inchmoan

South Beach

Inchgalbraith

Bandry Straits   **North**

Scale: 1 mile = 1.6km

Chart Eight - The 'Geggle' of Islands off Luss

The West Bank Northwards: Balloch to Luss

Balloch to Bandry Point (Chart Six)
Cameron House Hotel and Park

Cameron House and gardens, now a Leisure Centre and Marina, is also a unique starting point for exploring Lennox. In the hills above Cameron are the ruins of an iron-age hillfort, and Lang Cairn a neolithic chambered tomb, some 5,000 years old. Originally 200 yards long, the mound contained over twenty burials. It may also be the site of a battle between the Dalriadic Scots and the Cymric Britons in AD711. The *Annals* read "Conflict between the Britons and the Dalriads at Longecclet (Long Stones?) where the Britons were overcome."

Duck Bay Marina

Lying north of Cameron Point on the A82, the Marina, hotel and restaurant, provide every facility for the visitor and boating enthusiast. There is a licensed bar.

Temporary anchorage is available in the shallow waters north and south of the pier.

Auchenheglish

Situated a short distance below Nether-Ross Bay is Auchenheglish (Field of the Kirk), where the rocks and shoals offshore are believed to be the site of the old Kirk and Kirkyard, and where an iron cross was buried "deep in the loch" to mark the spot.

Loch Lomond Youth Hostel

The nearby Youth Hostel at Auchendennan is very popular, and the beautiful gardens of Auchendennan and Arden are well worth a visit.

Glen Fruin

The Fruin winds from the west, through the Glen, to emerge some three miles above Balloch, a half mile south-west of Inchmurrin. A monument marks the site of the famous conflict (or the infamous massacre) between the Macgregors and Colquhouns, which occurred in 1603. The final outcome was the suppression, and all but extinction, of the name MacGregor in 1664, but there is little doubt that the clan suffered blame for many actions that could well be laid on the Clan MacFarlane. The suppression was annulled in 1774.

The river is restricted to fly-fishing and salmon of around twenty pounds are occasionally caught on the Fruin.

Dumfin

Following the course of the Fruin westwards to Callendoon Bridge, on the summit of a round hill stand the ruins of an ancient hill-fort known as Dumfin (Fort of Finn), traditionally a stronghold and hunting-seat of Fingal (Finn McCoul, King of Morven), during the heroic but 'dark' ages. Several large bronze spearheads and ancient helmets were excavated on the lower slopes, a fact which lends some credence to the ancient legends.

Rossdhu

North of Glen Fruin is Rossdhu Point, with Rossdhu House and Deer Park (now a very select Golf Club) standing on the promontory of that name - Ross Dubh (Black Point). Rossdhu House was the seat of the Colquhoun Lairds of Luss for centuries, and the remains of the old family Chapel dating from the 12th century (where several splendid yew trees once grew), stand near the ruins of the ancient Castle of Rossdhu. Mary Queen of Scots was most hospitably entertained here. Alexander II of Scotland granted the Barony of Colquhoun to one Kilpatrick, whose successor, Ingram, took the surname of Colquhoun after marrying the 'Fair Maid of Luss', Rossdhu then became the seat of the family in the 13th century. Finlas Water divides the point, separating Rossdhu Park from the House and Golf Course.

Inland are several mesolithic remains, and a bronze-age site on Shantron Muir. In Auchentullich Bay between Midross Point and Rossdhu lies the McDougall Bank, an unmarked sandbank which should be carefully avoided at low water.

Bandry Point to Luss (Chart Seven)

St. Winifred's and St. Rosalind's

The A82 carries on towards Luss, passing alongside Camstradden Sound, which is entered via Bandry Strait. Off the south-west tip of Inchtavannach lies Eilean Dubh - 'Black Isle'. A typical islet, it is also named 'St. Winifred's' and due east nearby lies a submerged islet - 'St. Rosalind's'. Both were visible in 1827, when they were reported to be named after two sisters who picnicked here whilst staying for a time at Rossdhu House early in the eighteenth century.

Bandry Point and Straits to Camstradden Sound

At the southern entrance to the channel, the rocky shoals of Bandry Point jut out towards the south-western tip of Inchtavannach; the narrow passage between is marked by a buoy, and all boats are advised to steer carefully between the buoy and Inchtavannach! The shoals are the remains of a substantial piece of land, before rises in the Loch level eroded the soil away. Nearby the remains of the 'Cairn of Saint MacKessog' lay somewhere along the eighteenth century military road. It appears that the cairn was destroyed in the making of the road.

Rossarden Point and Bay

North of Bandry Strait, the promontory of Rossarden Point breaks the shoreline to add a little touch to the ever changing scenery in this picturesque channel, which is one of the most pleasant to sail through (excepting the Narrows on the other side of Inchtavannach). South of this, in Rossarden Bay below the Point, a stone pillar stands just offshore bearing the statue of a little boy. Known as 'Wee Peter' it is reputedly the work of a local boy who emigrated to Australia (where he became a sculptor), and who erected this during a subsequent return visit, to commemorate his childhood here. Another tale claims that it was erected in memory of a small boy who drowned there. As the latter, it is a reminder that the waters of Loch Lomond are not to be trifled with. An enigmatic '1890' is inscribed on the pillar, together with a later 'W. Kerr London 1904'.

Swan Island and Aldochlay Bay

Beyond Rossarden Point is Aldochlay Bay, a perfect haven for the many houseboats and other small craft moored there. It is also sheltered by a beautiful islet named Swan Island, probably the 'Ilan a Ghies an Shainie' (Isle of Swans of the Fairy-folk) of the 1701 list? This is an artificial 'crannog' island, and swans undoubtedly nest here as they do on other islands.

Camstradden Point

Excellent roofing slate was quarried at Camstradden for 400 years, and its slate of deep-blue was highly valued. Slate Bay forms an area of open water before Camstradden Point, projecting from which is a submerged promontory described as an island by Camden (1586) - four centuries ago. On it stood an orchard, garden and house, situated there in his lifetime.

Luss

The A82 now comes to this attractive area and a new perspective of the Loch opens up; and a new Visitor Centre.

There is little to add to the existing descriptions of Luss, the most picturesque village on the Loch; the surrounding countryside equally fascinating and home ground to the clan Colquhoun; the hills resplendent with oak, ash, holly, rowan, birch, hazel, aspen, and alder. Good shallow water anchorage may be had on each side of the pier. Part of the road to the old slate quarries at Camstradden was constructed by 'Colonel Lascelle's Regiment May 1745'. and a milestone three miles from Luss is so inscribed.

Follow the spawning sea-trout and salmon up the course of Luss Water, and past the church, where ancient stone coffins (cut from the solid rock) were discovered many years ago. Several hundred yards upstream the old slate-banks are evident everywhere, and in this vicinity lies a most enchanting glade. Best seen when the sun is shining directly from its westward trajectory, a natural bathing pool is surrounded by natural benches of sandy to light-green slate, unlike the light to dark-blue slate quarried at Camstradden. The pool appears almost circular, with crystal-clear water enlivening the smooth slate-clad floor. When the sun shines directly downstream the trees and sloping banks come alive with fairy-like motes in its beams, while the different shades of slate present a beautiful pastel mosaic on the bottom of the pool. Many shades hover in the sunbeams, along with the dancing specks. Neolithic flint implements have been discovered in Glen Luss.

Some three and a half miles further up, the name of Luss Water changes to 'Gleann ma Caoruinn' where are the ruins of a village which once supported a weaving community. A few tumbled headstones in the graveyard remain the only link with its past.

The sculptured stones found around Luss old church are typically Celtic in form, although derived from the so-called 'Govan School' several distinctions are to be found. The interlace may be of Cymric/Anglian origin, with Scandinavian elements. Certain motifs are Irish, while others are of undeniably Pictish origin. On the whole they reflect an early Christian art resulting from much intercourse between cultures, and therefore represent the sacred nature of the Loch itself.

Once named 'Clachan Dubh' - Black Village (a poor misnomer, and a possible confusion with an abandoned village higher up the Loch), Luss is said to have received this name due to an early dusk which falls when the sun slips below the high hills behind, and the village does lose the sun an hour or two earlier in the evening. In the Gaelic 'Lus' describes a plant or herb, or a garden, and one source claims that the name derives from the fragrant herbs (which took root here) used to embalm the body of St. Kessog. Another source claims that 'Lus' derives from the 'fleur-de-Lys' brought from France (c1795) with the body of the Baroness MacAuslan who is buried in the churchyard. Yet another source renders 'L-u-s' into some ancient hero, and a Scandinavian source translates it as 'bright and clear'.

King Robert the Bruce and his followers hunted their food in the surrounding hills during their march to Dumbarton after his defeat at Methven in 1306, a debt he repaid in full at Bannockburn eight years later. He also repaid a debt to Luss when he granted a charter to John of Luss (1292-1333), "for the reverance and honour of our patron, the most holy man, the blessed Kessog." And in 1323 he granted a sanctuary girth of three miles to the church of Luss - "to God and the blessed Kessog".

The various Colquhoun Lairds of Luss appear to have been singularly unfortunate on their home ground for Sir John was killed by the islanders of Inchmurrin in 1417, while the Governor of Dumbarton Castle, another Sir John, was killed in its defence in 1478. In 1592 Sir Humphrey Colquhoun was killed at his castle of Bandry by an arrow supposed at the time shot by a MacGregor or a MacFarlane, but later found to have been his own bowmen at the instigation of his brother. Edinburgh records for November 1592 state:- "Jon Cachoune was beheedit for murthering his ane brother the Laird of Luss".

The Gaelic was commonly spoken here some 150 years ago, and it was noted in 1839 that "there are seven public houses in the Parish. Their effect is decidedly unfavourable!"

The 'Geggle' of Islands off Luss (Chart Eight)

Inchcruin is the first island in this cluster known as the 'Geggle' when leaving Inchcailleach and Inchfad behind, cruising the islands from Balmaha. westwards towards Luss.

Inchcruin

'Yniscruny' the so-called 'Round Island' (one 18th century account translates this 'island of Picts' another names it 'Big Ireland' from 'Cruithne' - both correct), is the most westerly of the islands lying within the Stirlingshire boundary. Inchcruin forms the eastern 'leg' of the U-shaped Geggle which includes Inchmoan and Inchconnachan, and it is possible to wade across the shallow sandbank between Inchcruin (reputed to have been used as an asylum for the mentally deranged), and Inchmoan. Inchcruin is a half-mile long, and over a quarter-mile broad; to the south and a quarter-mile off Inchfad to the east is a good fishing area for sea-trout and salmon. Larch trees grow here, and two crannogs lie half-submerged off the south shore, with another towards Bucinch. Several large rocks lie to the north-west and south. Two small bays with beaches, and another larger, with a private jetty to the farmhouse, lie facing east towards Milarrochy Bay. Other bays and beaches may be found on the west and south shores.

Bucinch

From 'Yla nam bock' of 1656 - Island of Cattle, or Goats. Covered with Scots firs, this dome-headed island lying to the north of Inchcruin was inhabited until recently, and the house is still there. A stone stands on the east bank in memory of four men from the Clyde shipyards who drowned early this century.

Ceardach

Ceardach - 'the Smithy' - is an islet east of Bucinch covered in vegetation and containing unexcavated remains; many burnt stones indicate this might have been the site of a metalworker. This is the last island lying within the Stirlingshire boundary with Dunbartonshire. Bucinch and Ceardach are National Trust of Scotland property, and access is limited.

Inchmoan

Here, on a sun-kissed crescent of clean yellow sand, in water clear as crystal, sunbathing and swimming is pleasurable and safe. the clean sandy bottom is visible for some two hundred yards out, and the depth no more than five or six feet for over one hundred! This magnificent beach is one of four or five on the island of Inchmoan or 'Island of Peat', three-quarters of a mile long, one quarter wide, lying northwest of Inchcailleach's Portbawn and almost centre in the cluster of islands between Balmaha and the village of Luss to the west. Another large beach lies on the north side.

Little of Inchmoan's history is recorded, except that it provided a supply of peat-fuel for the villagers of Luss, while the ruins of a building surrounded by Scots fir-trees at the western tip are reputed to have been a house of correction, where the people of Luss appear to have exiled their habitual drunkards and ladies of doubtful virtue.

One memorably hot day on the golden beach, the boat people were mostly sunbathing, while the youngsters played in the shallows and the boats lay motionless at anchor. A small powerboat came to rest on the beach and disgorged two curvy young ladies in bikinis who promptly spread blankets or towels and lay down to sunbathe. A very strange phenomena then occurred, before long the hitherto comatose male population (9/10) began strolling nonchalantly, in twos and threes, back and forth along the water's edge near the new arrivals; almost as at some telepathically communicated signal. The ladies had, it seems, mistaken the beach for that of a (mythical?) nudist club and were, naturally, sunbathing accordingly! They soon realised their mistake and hastily fled, to the chagrin of the now fully mobilised males.

Inch Galbraith

Just off the southwest point of Inchmoan, and within swimming distance, lies Inch Galbraith. A man-made crannog, the islet contains ruins of one of the principal Galbraiths strongholds. The Galbraith name is from the Gaelic 'Gallbreagha' - Clan Briton - of ancient origin. They flourished between the 12th and 16th centuries, holding lands in the Lennox area. Culcreuch Castle near Fintry (now a popular hotel and country park) was once a stronghold of Thomas, 12th 'chieffe of the Galbraiths', who was hanged by James IV in 1489 for his part in the battle of Talla-Moss (near Touch, Stirling), an event which ended the rebellion led by the Earl of Lennox. Inch Galbraith was a substantial island in earlier times, when water level was lower.

The Galbraiths seem to have forfeited most of their lands by 1630, when Inch Galbraith was, presumably, abandoned. Ospreys bred annually on the islet until the last breeding pair were shot by colonel John Colquhoun around 1825 - "when still in his youth", and it is written that "he bitterly regretted this act of folly ever afterwards." The north shores of Inchmoan sheltered by islands east and west provide good fishing, though this area, the main part of The Geggle, is also a popular spot for water-skiers. the northern beach almost equals the southern 'Golden Crescent' in popularity. Sea-trout and salmon are caught offshore to the south-west, in a triangular area formed by Rossdhu and Bandry on the mainland, and Inch Galbraith.

Stot Island

This shallow, willow-grown bank, jutting from south Inchtavannach towards Inchmoan, is marked by a warning post. It may have been regarded as a 'floating island' in the past, due to the rise in the water level (2.5 metres/8.2feet), during the Spring floods, when only the outermost tip (marked by a beacon) remained above water.

Boaters are advised that there is a water-speed limit of 5 miles per hour here in the Straits, and 'Friends of the Loch' observe it. Waves from a fast power-boat do erode the island shores.

Ilan an Imrich

This is 'Floating Island' a seemingly moving islet at the entrance to the Narrows, off Inconnachan. A simple grass and shingle bank, old sources name this one of the three wonders of the Loch, "Waves without winds fish without fins, and a floating Island".

The fact is that Imrich disappears when the water rises, at which point Stot Island seems to distance itself further from Inchtavannach, and move closer to Inchconnachan.

Inchconnachan

Lying almost parallel, and east of Inchtavannach, 'Inchcalloun' (Inchconacher's or Colquhoun's) Isle is three-quarters of a mile long, a quarter mile wide, and 200ft/61m at the highest point. It forms the western leg of The Geggle, which includes Inchmoan and Inchcruin. Together with the unrivalled magic of the Narrows she shares with Inchtavannach on her western shore, she almost surpasses and is certainly as beautiful as her sister island; with rocky promontories, indented gravel beaches and large groups of magnificent and ancient Scottish firs. Prehistoric remains lie at the north-eastern tip. The Galbraiths of Bandry and Castelgill (Castle Galbraith) also established themselves here in early times.

Lady Arran (the intrepid first lady of powerboat racing) established a badger retreat on Inchconnachan, and also introduced the wallaby (a small kangaroo), and a peccary (a semi-wild pig-like animal from South America). Passing one of the tiny beaches one day, we noticed two families, scurrying back to their beached cruisers, to peer anxiously back into the trees beyond the beach, where the little peccary gazed back at them forlornly. During a jaunt on the island we too came face to face with this small beastie, and soon discovered that he was lonely and simply seeking company of any kind.

The secluded bay facing Inchmoan's north-western tip provides a popular anchorage known as The Haven. Many impromptu barbecues and sing-songs to the accompaniment of guitar and/or other instrument have been enjoyed around a campfire, beneath the magnificence of the few remaining ancient Scottish firs. Once so abundant here, and as on other islands, they are now unfortunately seriously endangered, reduced by storm and the encroachment of the water. However, while storms may be blamed for a number, many trees have been killed off by the insane practice of lighting fires in the lee of the trunk at the base.

One summer we climbed the southern peak of Inchconnachan from the east bank in the Straits, the hot and humid atmosphere among the tumbled boulders and fallen tress conjuring images of some primeval forest. We rested on a rock formation by a tiny pool on top, in a natural basin of rock, with an armchair shaped protrusion that fitted me admirably. The peaceful air and magnificent view enforced relaxation until, on rising, using the right 'arm' of the 'chair' I noticed a slight movement. A hairline crack appeared across the top, another along a straition several inches below. For some reason we lifted this wedge-shaped chunk and saw what seemed to be a 'black-hole' (the only suitable description). Within seconds, the 'thing' appeared to sprout legs and promptly hopped over the rock to disappear into the pool below! A small, shallow, saucer-like hollow, lined with barely visible fine moss lay surrounded by the newly exposed grey granite and quartz of which Inchconnachan is mostly composed. There was no sign of a fissure, crack, or any opening by which means the 'toad' (or indeed anything) might enter. Many stories of 'toads' imprisoned in apparently solid rock have been recorded over the centuries, and though these are invariably discredited by scientists, nonetheless, the feeling that some kind of 'Pandora's Box' had been opened remains.

The Straits and Narrows

There are several 'Straits' in the area, one is the narrow passage between Inchtavannach's south-west tip, and Bandry Point, the next is one between Inchmoan's south-western tip and Inchtavannach; another between Inchmoan's north-west tip and Inchconnachan. The last two open into a placid expanse which leads into the exquisite Narrows. This entrancing waterway between Inchtavannach and Inchconnachan is arguably best cruised from the south, and requires careful navigation by all boats except those of very shallow-draught, owing to a number of submerged rocks and the nature of its narrow winding course. A careful and leisurely cruise is well rewarded, and towards evening, when the sun is beginning its descent, an almost mystical quality imbues the more receptive with a sense that the spirit of Merlin himself might hover over the reed-banks and lillies, where the swans often feed at leisure. There are many places on the Loch where this almost magical aura surrounds the area.

A small, secluded and sheltered inlet with a shingle beach on Inchtavannach near the northern exit/entrance to the Narrows, is a popular picnic ground for fishermen and sailing families alike.

Inchtavannach

Across the Narrows from Inchconnachan lies Inchtavannach. Her high (340ft/104m) wooded-slopes a true haunt of Sylvanus, she derives her name from the Gaelic 'Ilan de Mhonach' or Norse-Gaelic 'Innis tigh Manach', Isle of Monks or Isle of the House of Monks respectively. Both are correct, for it was here, where the present farmhouse stands, that St. Kessog, patron saint of Luss, built his 'monastery' in the 6th century. A 13th century chartulary names this 'Inesdomhnoch'. Few visible signs remain, but subsequent archaeology may yet reveal the bee-hive cells of these early Christians, and several ancient stones have been uncovered in the past.

A mile long and some half-mile wide the island is undoubtedly the most striking of this eastern Geggle and its magnificent ancient Firs and

Oaks, the lush vegetation, sand and shingle banks, and numerous sheltered inlets are prominent features. The lovely Roe-deer once roamed this beautiful island.

On top of 'Tom nan Clag' - the Knoll of the Bell, at the northern high point, St. Kessog is believed to have rung his bell to call the new faithful to prayer. The hill takes its name from the ancient Celtic bells (shaped like antique sheet-iron cow-bells) carried by the early Christian missionaries to the Picts, Scots and Britons of the area, and St. Kessog's was still be be seen in the late seventeenth century, held in great reverence by the people of the Lennox. Similar bells may be seen in the national museums, encased in richly decorated shrines of gold, silver and enamels; associated with various saints.

One of the earliest of missionaries, St. Kessog was martyred c560 AD near Bandry Strait at the southern end of Camstradden Sound. An effigy from the 12/14th century Chapel at Rossdhu now stands in Luss Church. 'Tom nan Clag' is more likely named from its bell-like outline when viewed from a distance, and so it truly is, 'Machessog's Bell'.

Visitors to the top of the hill are rewarded with a panoramic and breathtaking view of the Loch, while the slopes are home to many jackdaws and the occasional hawk-type bird. The Capercaillie (the cock o' the woods) is often seen among the trees. Inchtavannach is on record in 1492 when 'Instavanhoe and Castillgill' (Inch Galbraith) were granted to a Napier of Merchiston, an ancestor of the Napier to whom science owes the Logarithms and the decimal point.

Oaks - Heather - Cormorants and Black Rocks

Cruising north past Camstradden Point (or through the Narrows) a short distance away lie the twin Islets of Daraich (Oak Island, a nesting place for Tern and Black-headed Gulls) and Craoibhe (Isle of the Tree). Midway between these and Heather Isle is a safe passage to Luss Bay. 'Fraoch Eilean' - 'Freuchlan' or Fern Isle was once noted as a "reformatory for the erring wives of Luss". It is regarded as one of the most beautiful of all islands, though small, and ravaged by a fire which destroyed her venerable Scots firs many years ago, she is entirely feminine. With her smoothly moulded and softly folded rock flowing in numerous ripples, she yet retains a gem-like quality in her exquisitely faceted form, while her drapery is laced with the various colours of the heather and the ferns.

The passages on either side of Heather Isle should be navigated with care at low water level, while good fishing is to be had off the eastern banks. Between here and Inchlonaig lie the Cargiedows, 'Creagan Dubha' Black Rocks, the most prominent is 'Creag nan sgarth' or 'Cormorant's Rock' which they still favour as a perch. The nearest to Luss is 'Carraig an Dubh' Black Rock.

West Bank: Northwards from Luss to Ardlui

Leaving Luss Bay, and passing the sand and shingle beaches of Rhu Camp-site off Rhu Wood, just over a mile brings us to Culag, from where Isles of Ross and Point of Ross on the east bank lie three-quarters of a mile away, while another mile and a half further north is Inverbeg.

Inverbeg (Chart Two)
Inverbeg lies at the mouth of Douglas Water, and the renowned Inverbeg Hotel is a popular resort of the angling fraternity. A ferry regularly plies between here and Rowardennan. Inland, in Glen Douglas, old traditions have it that King Arthur once came here with an army of Britons from Strathclyde and fought a mighty battle with the Picts and Scots, before also defeating the army brought by the King of Ireland (Guilamurius) to aid these invaders. It is said that the Picts and Scots retreated to the various islands, where he pursued and "slew them in their thousands". Well! Dumbarton Rock was once named 'Castrum Arthuri' in the Public Records!

The Fairy Loch to Tarbet (Chart Three)
A mile or so beyond Inverbeg, and before Rubha Mor (Great Point), lies Lochan Uaine the almost legendary Fairy Loch. It takes just a short climb inland to reveal this enchanted spot. Though hidden from view by the ascent from the loch, the climb is most rewarding. Even the trees surrounding this liquid jewel seem to hold something fairy-like in their branches as they bow in homage to the kaleidoscope of rainbow colours which imbue the water when the sunbeams play across its surface. The lochan (small lake) was reputed to have supplied local weavers with the

dyes for their products until the spell was broken by a wicked witch who asked the ariels to change her black cloth to white. It was (and may still be!) a romantic spot for lovers, and visitors still throw pennies into the water for future luck and happiness.

From Rubha Mor, several pleasant little bays provide the sailor with good anchorage. North is Firkin Point, then the Firkin Tollbar, and Robert the Bruce's Tree, under which the hero sheltered for a while after the affair at Dalrigh in 1603. Both are situated inland just above 'Stuc an-t Iobhairt'. Next on the A82 isRubha Dubh (Black-point), then Rubha Ban (White-point), and another half a mile Stuckgowan

Clachan Dubh

Lying in the hills above Stuckgowan are the desolate ruins of the village Clachan Dubh, or Black Village, where the population was wiped out by plague many years ago. The plague originated in the Middle-east, arriving in Scotland around Columba's time along with early Christian missionaries from North Africa; and the many early Christian sites around attest to the evidence for this ancient sacred attachment to Loch Lomond. The plague visited Scotland during the years 550 - 580 - 664 -1350 - 1569 - 1650 and 1894.

Tarbet and Tarbet Isle

Another mile brings the visitor to Tarbet (Draw-pass), where in 1263 Norwegian marauders under Olaf of Man (allied to Haco of Norway) drew no less than 60 galleys across the narrow isthmus between Arrochar on Loch Long, and Tarbet; almost one and a quarter miles. From here they launched a dreadful assault on the Loch, "wasting the populous islands, the strengths and villages along its banks". They paid dearly for this raid however, for they lost ten boats to a storm on Loch Fyne before rejoining Haco's fleet. Then all were swept to destruction at the Battle of Largs.

There is a pier, an excellent hotel, a post office, a general store, and a garage where fuel is obtained. Tarbet Isle is a beautifully wooded islet half a mile north.

Inveruglas to Ardlui (Chart Four)

Coasting on, passing Blairannaich and Kenmore Wood brings us to Inveruglas river, bay, hotel, and ferry from Inversnaid. High in the hills above lies Loch Sloy (Loch of the Host), once gathering place for the Clan MacFarlane; also their slogan or war-cry. It now supplies energy to the Power Station below, and the huge pipes carrying its water scar the natural beauty of the western banks.

The larger island at the mouth of Inveruglas Water is Wallace's Isle reputed to have sheltered the fugitive Scottish hero before his seizure in 1305. This was achieved by the treachery of John Short, a servant, who betrayed him to Sir John Mentieth, castellan of Dunbarton- who handed him to England's King Edward to whom most Scottish nobles had earlier sworn an Oath of Allegiance.

On Inveruglas Island (situated in the bay just north of Inveruglas Water), lie the ruins of another keep of the MacFarlanes. The Isle was once one of their principal strongholds, and the castle considered powerful and dangerous enough to be sacked by Cromwell's troops in 1650. It was completely abandoned by 1785.

From here and dark Isle I Vow, the MacFarlanes raided the southern mainlands, their nocturnal activities aided by a bright moon; and a visit under the moonlight of 'MacFarlane's Lantern' could still conjure up startling visions of their martial comings and goings.

Ardvorlich Bay, Guy Rock and Pulpit Rock

On northwards, this enchanting little bay provides excellent anchorage, and is surrounded by pleasant wooded hills and gentle slopes which provide protection from south and west. A large cairn (Cean More), a prehistoric burial mound, protects the bay on the east.

This is undoubtedly the best base from which to explore Isle I Vow, a short distance away north-east by small boat. Between, and slightly east, is submerged Guy Rock possibly an islet before the water rose. Half a mile above I Vow is the massive sculptured rock known as Pulpit Rock past Rubha Ban Point. It once had a strong door to the steps chiselled in the rock, and it is possible that many early Christians heard the Word of God, together with many denouncements against the heathen Picts to the east, from this ancient place. Another half mile north is Stuckindroin where the round Burial Mounds are claimed to be the largest in the country. The presence of a number of submerged rocks and shoals in the vicinity of Rubha Ban suggest the location of one of several 'lost' islands - Ilan Nemheann - The Heavenly Isle , though this has been tentatively located at the mouth of the River Falloch.

Ardlui

The pier provides safe anchorage on either side, and small craft may moor on the river banks. There is a fine hotel with gardens, a public telephone, shop and caravan site; Crianlarich is some eight miles further on the A82.

The Enchanted Loch

Loch Lomond is undoubtedly enchanted in summer and I am eternally grateful for the many idyllic summers we were fortunate enough to spend there. During those halcyon days our regular anchorage lay in a tiny inlet on the east bank of Inchtavannach, in the channel entered from The Geggle and separating it from Inchconnachan, at the entrance to the The Straits or Narrows and well sheltered from contrary winds. Weekends usually began on Friday evening, when, with her moorings at Balmaha left astern the boat seemed to surge along of its own volition, as if impatient to reach our little haven. From here we could visit the other islands, or villages, or simply sail around enjoying the ever-changing vistas which presented themselves.

One memorable evening, we anchored for the night at the north end of Camstradden Sound, in Slate Bay on the west banks of the loch, with Inchtavannach just across the water. It was almost dusk, that eerie half-light when the spirits conjure up tricks to beguile human imagination; no breath of air rippled the water, nothing disturbed the tranquil scene. Then **HE** arrived! A raucous call echoed along the channel between the wooded slopes and the mainland, the noise emanating from a small object winging and weaving an erratic flight towards us. Finally, appeared a large duck, which suddenly swooped, as if afraid of overshooting, hit the water and almost tumbled tail over beak in its haste to reach us. We were to learn that this was one of his better landings. Once orientated he splashed, flapped and squawked his way to the boat, undoubtedly saying "I'm hungry". Apparently satisfied with the bread and biscuits given him he quietly paddled his way around the boat in a most peculiar manner. His head bobbed and twisted as he inspected the vessel, as if assessing our suitability for adoption. We named him 'Kwackers'!

The one-eyed duck back-pedals before making one of his usual, and highly amusing landings. Splashing down in a great flurry of water he would then weave his way to the boat like a drunken sailor trying to walk on water. Quacking and squawking noisily in an unmistakable call for his supper!

We awoke the following morning to an incessant tap-tapping on the hull. Visions of dragging anchors and a jagged slate bottom created a minor panic. It was merely our friend of the night before announcing breakfast time. Needless to say, his fast was broken long before ours. He had only one eye, which accounted for his peculiar movements and splash-downs. He woke us every morning in the same manner, and after a day out on the loch he would greet our return at dusk just as he had done the first time. That is, until one balmy evening when the familiar squawk did not sound over the water and he too, like Pat of Portbawn, failed to reappear. We never saw him again and strongly suspect he fell foul of some crass 12 bore(e)ing sportsman. A little of the mystery, some of the strange and almost magical influence of the loch went with him.

One door had closed when Kwackers disappeared, but another opened in our anchorage at the approach to the Narrows. We were adopted again, by a pair of swans. The large male, beautiful and graceful as his mate, was much bolder, and once again we began to receive regular visitors. Soon, even his timid mate would take food from the hand, and one annual event they shared with us was most enchanting of all.

The pair nested among the reeds on a spit of land jutting from Inchconnachan opposite, and the treat they provided in return for a few items of food was extremely rewarding. Each year they entertained us with their regular family parades. The recently arrived cygnets, exquisite despite their scruffy grey-brown livery, would scuttle along behind majestic mum and dad in a stately though disorderly procession; cruising back and forth in zig-zagging toward the boat with no little display of pride. The clutch varied from four to seven and we suspected that the huge pike inhabiting the loch hereabouts caught one or two during their early days. They grew all too quickly and soon flew away on their own individual quests.

One season, after a year's absence, we decided to relax on a small mainland beach; an excuse for sampling the fare at a nearby hostelry. A sudden flurry of activity roused us from the lethargy of sunbathing and we were alarmed to see people scattering in all directions, away from the water's edge. How easily panic and near hysteria spreads! We too joined the retreating crowd in the rush from the water, only to halt as realisation came. We were actually running away from a very special friend! Away from a large swan which, with its great wings spread wide and hissing loudly (as folk said), had come ashore and was running towards us! I turned around much too late. The noble creature was already walking slowly back to the water. There was a certain something in the way he bore himself; an air of rejection? I had missed an ideal opportunity to prove our mutual trust. One observer later remarked on the fact that the swan had stopped for a moment by the rug we had left behind on the sand and had paused before turning away from the spot we had so thoughtlessly and hastily vacated.

The swans continued to visit us, but the relationship was never quite the same, and a season or so later the female disappeared. The lone male hung around for a time and rarely came to the boat, then he too was gone. We thought we heard music for several evenings; a barbecue on another island, or swan song. Although other swans inhabit the loch, our anchorage and its proximity to one particular nest had made us trusted neighbours. Mute swans do make sounds, they hiss, it's the only sound they make, and the memory of a broken trust lingers; though perhaps this thought is mere presumption.

The Loch is always enchanted, and I hope the preceding pages may enable others to see the special magic of this 'Marvel of Britain'.

A Literary Association

Dorothy Wordsworth penned a number of verses on Loch Lomond in her *Memorials of a Tour in Scotland* . One, entitled 'The Brownie's Cell' refers to a "lonely little Isle" (I Vow) whereon lay a "consecrated Pile" destroyed by "servants of another world with madding Power" where, "a Wretch retired - Proud Remnant of a fearless Race". The poetess compares this hermit with the Patmos Saint (St. John the Apostle), and has him writing the "faded glories of his Clan". In the last verse, the Isle is a "Wild Relique! beauteous as Nysa's Isle where Bacchus was conveyed - to lie". He may have been the author of a Scottish geographical manuscript.

Wordsworth later added a sequel verse named 'The Brownie' in which she describes the solitary end of this member of the Clan MacFarlane who distinguished themselves at Flodden and Pinkie, and fought for Montrose. Like the MacGregors, their name was all but extinguished and many survivors changed the name. Their principal crime appears to have been the killing of Colquhoun of Luss in 1608. Cattle-raiding was a way of life, and most clan feuds were invariably machinated by political and court intrigues. Bowmen support the Arms of MacFarlane, which could settle the name of Isle I Vow as the 'Isle of the Bow'.

The Scottish 'Brownie' was a benevolent spirit, assuming the form of a tall young man who laboured the various tasks, usually that of cleaning a house and its surroundings for little more than a bite to eat. The early description of Isle I Vow as "a pretty good house with gardens" would seem to identify its solitary occupant as the 'Brownie' - one determined to preserve this edifice of his race in stone, flowers and the pen. There may be a possible confusion, however, with Inveruglas Island, attacked and destroyed by Cromwell's soldiers.

Loch Lomond undoubtedly inspired the poet, and one verse has supplied us with a most appropriate symbol for this 'star' of lochs -"To the Planet Venus, an Evening Star".

Note. For a comprehensive survey and information on literary associations *see* Louis Stott's *Ring of Words. Literary Loch Lomond. 1995*

42

An Old Historical Association

A disparate name for the Loch is given in Richard of Cirencester's work 'De Situ Britanniae' attributed to the fourteenth century, though some other authorities claim it to be a work of the sixteenth, or even eighteenth. The name seems to be hybrid from 'Leine Celidon' or 'Lein Calder', 'Lake of Caledonia' or 'fast-flowing water' both equating with the Vale of Leven, the Lennox; and possibly Elizabethan. The publishing of Spenser's sixth book of the 'Faerie Queene' and the outbreak of war in Ireland against Tyrone and his Spaniards in 1598, coincided with the mass hastening north of English courtiers to woo James VI, whom they felt certain was the future King of England.

Richard refers to it as 'Lyncalidor' the Lake of Calidor, and when Spenser began his 'Faerie Queene' he intended twelve books; each named after a knight of specific virtue and Arthurian in character. The sixth book concerns the 'Knight of Courtesie' = 'Sir Calidore' - whose quest was to vanquish the 'Blatant Beast' of fifty thousand tongues; a dragon pouring forth foul slander (very plentiful in 1598).

Allegorically, the character of Calidore has been applied to Sir Philip Sidney, and to the Earl of Essex, both of whom were consummate courtiers. But both incurred the Queen's displeasure around this time, and when Richard's placing of Lyncalidor is taken into consideration, the most suitable character is Ludovic Stuart, the 2nd Duke of Lennox (1583/1624). First favourite of King James VI and I, he was also highly thought of by Queen Elizabeth, for whom he offered to lead an army of Scots against Tyrone in Ireland. Elizabeth replied that she could "never hazard so valuable a life in so perilous an enterprise" thus he was highly esteemed at Elizabeth's Court. Exceptionally striking in figure, he was educated at the French court (of Courtesy) and heir presumptive to James VI. He was also third in line to the English Crown! Lennox therefore had these advantages over Essex, 'The Lake of the Knight of Courtesie' was Loch Lomond, Lennox's domain there. the 'Blatant Beast' the tongues of rumour; scurrilous tales of James' relationship with Lennox's father.

References and Further Reading

Anderson, J. - Scotland in Early Christian Times, 1880, and Scotland in Pagan Times. 1883

Burn, A. R. - Holy Men on Islands in Pre-Christian Britain. *Archaeological Journal of Ireland* 1969

Calendar of State Papers, 1569-1603

Camden, WM. Britannia 1586

Chambers, Robert - Domestic Annals of Scotland 1874

Eyre-Todd, G. with **E. W. Haslehust** - Loch Lomond, Loch Katrine and the Trossachs 1922

Fraser, Sir William - The Lennox. 1874

Friends of Loch Lomond - Newsletters; Reports; and Archaeological Survey

Geikie, Sir A. - History of Scotland. 1901

Glasgow University - A Natural History of Loch Lomond. 1974, reprint 1990, by Loch Lomond Park Authority

Iona Club - Collectanea De Rebus Albanicis incl. Annals of the Four Masters, 1860s

Irving, J. - History of Dunbartonshire. 1924

Lacaille, A. - Stone Age Scotland. 1854

Lamond, H. - Loch Lomond. 1931

Lindsay, R. - History and Chronicles of Scotland 1500s

Loch Lomond Park Authority - Reports; Ranger Series; Guides; Registration and Navigation Bye-laws, 1995; Guide to Navigation 1996; *Natural History of Loch Lomond* (reprint)

Loch Lomond Association- Newsletters; Code of Conduct

MacGregor, A.A. - Wild Drumalbain 1927

MacGregore, Sir James. Book of the Dean of Lismore, Scottish Verse. 1937 ed by Wilson.

MacGregor, Jimmie - On the West Highland Way. 1985

Miller & Tivy - The Glasgow Region, The British Association survey 1954.

Munro, R. - Ancient Scottish Lake Dwellings. 1882

Murray, W.M.M., Rob Roy MacGregor, 1982.

Nature Conservancy Council - Loch Lomond Nature Reserve, Inchcailleach

Nimmo, W. History of Stirlingshire - 3rd edition, 2 vols. 1880

Pennant, T. - Tours in Scotland. 1760 and 1772, 3 vols. 1790

Richard of Cirencester - De Situ Britanniae - attributed to 14th C

Royal Commission for Ancient Monuments. Stirlingshire inventory, 2 vols. 1964.

Sankey, Steven - Loch Lomond Landscapes. 1985

Scottish Council for National Parks - Submission to the Loch Lomond Working Party 1992

Skene, W.F. - Celtic Scotland, 1876, and Chronicles of the Picts and Scots. 1867

Statistical Account for Scotland, 1791/1845/1966. Stirlingshire and Dunbartonshire parishes

Stott, L. - Ring of Words. Literary Loch Lomond. 1995

Thomas, A.C. - The Early Christian Archaeology of North Britain. 1971

Weir, Tom - Scottish Lochs, 1970

Wordsworth, W. - Tour in Scotland. 1814